coffee
SCRUMPTIOUS DRINKS AND TREATS

By Betty Rosbottom

Photographs by Lara Hata

CHRONICLE BOOKS
SAN FRANCISCO

ISBN 10: 0-8118-5237-7
ISBN 13: 978-0-8118-5237-1

Manufactured in China.

Design and typesetting by Carole Goodman,
   Blue Anchor Design
Food styling by George Dolese
Assistant photography by Aaron Fee, Ha Huynh,
   and Brian Slaughter
Assistant food styling by Elisabet der Nederlanden

10 9 8 7 6 5 4 3 2 1

Chronicle Books LLC
85 Second Street
San Francisco, California 94105

www.chroniclebooks.com

DEDICATION

For the caffeinated crew who worked so hard with me on this book:
Emily, Sheri, Deb, Ellen, Jane, and Barbara

ACKNOWLEDGMENTS

This book could not have been written without the help of a small and very talented group of women. Emily Bell and Sheri Lisak, my longtime friends and collaborators, once again shared their talents and enthusiasm for yet another of my projects. Deb Brown worked tirelessly by my side to develop and create recipes day after day, week after week. Barbara O'Connor and Jane Giat made many recipes better with their suggestions. Ellen Ellis, gifted writer and cook, spent countless hours helping me research the history of coffee.

Wendy Gabriel, friend and assistant, stepped in at the last minute to test some final creations for this collection.

My agent, Judith Weber, as always, offered encouragement and good counsel, and Leslie Jonath, editor at Chronicle Books, first proposed the idea of a coffee book. Thanks to Laurel Leigh for expertly overseeing the production of this book, to copyeditor Ann Martin Rolke for her astute eye, to Lara Hata for the beautiful photographs, and to Carole Goodman for the enticing design for this collection.

Finally, thanks to my husband, Ron, who gives his support in so many ways, even when it means critiquing an espresso martini at 9 o'clock in the morning!

TABLE OF CONTENTS

INTRODUCTION

AS A YOUNGSTER, I REMEMBER BEING AWAKENED BY THE SOUNDS OF A household coming to life—the hiss of bacon frying, the cracking of eggs, and the chortling of the percolator. Many distinctive kitchen aromas wafted into my room, but more than anything else, it was the deep, rich scent of freshly brewed coffee that made me rise. Once I arrived at the breakfast table, my mother would offer me what Southerners refer to as "milk-coffee"—a cup filled with steaming hot milk, a heaping teaspoon of sugar, and just a touch of the morning brew.

My college memories are also scented with coffee, although by the time I arrived at Newcomb College at Tulane, my morning cup of coffee had taken on normal proportions. By then I was sipping on rich dark coffee splashed with milk or cream. My roommates and I brewed pot after pot of coffee in an effort to stay awake and to appear worldly. On many occasions, we ventured into New Orleans' French Quarter, where we dipped hot beignets into the city's special chicory-laced coffee. As a junior, I went off to Paris for a year of study abroad, and my coffee repertoire expanded. My day began with café au lait, a soulful drink of steamy milk and coffee, and often ended with a demitasse of espresso.

Newly married, I progressed from making coffee in a percolator to using a filter-style drip pot. When entertaining, I brewed coffee in an elegant cafetière, or plunger pot, and also turned out espresso in a moka espresso pot.

What a joy it has been for me to revisit so many of these moments as I worked on this book about coffee. On the following pages, you'll find the directions for all manner of coffee drinks as well as recipes for a delectable array of sweet treats to accompany this beloved brew. I agree with that anonymous wise soul who said, "A cup of coffee with a friend is happiness tasted and time well spent." I hope you'll enjoy, then, making and sharing these coffee drinks and confections with others.

—*Betty Rosbottom*

COFFEE BEANS

There are two basic types of coffee beans: *robusta* and *arabica*. Robusta coffee is the less expensive of the two. It is grown at lower elevations, is highly caffeinated, and has an astringent flavor. Arabica coffee is a superior grade, and almost two-thirds of the coffee growers of the world cultivate this type of bean. Arabica beans contain about half the caffeine of robusta. Amongst arabica coffees, there are many subtle differences. However, the arabica beans can be broadly characterized by their growing regions. Beans from Latin America, for example, are typically a bit sweet and highly acidic and are often described as "subtle but crisp." Beans from the Pacific, such as Kona beans, are smooth, gentle, and mild, while Sumatran beans are distinguished by their full-bodied earthiness. Many canned coffees sold in supermarkets are a blend of both robusta and arabica beans.

Caffeinated vs. Decaffeinated Beans

The same caffeinated coffee that you start your day with may interfere with a good night's sleep, so a decaffeinated variety is a good alternative for later hours in the day. Coffee beans can be decaffeinated by two different processes. One is known as the Swiss water process, and the other as the direct contact method. The latter is usually considered to yield a more flavorful cup. As a general rule when brewing decaffeinated coffee, invest in the best decaffeinated beans you can find, and do not grind them until brewing time.

ROASTING

Roasting is said to have begun in Ethiopia in the thirteenth century, and while there have been many attempts to perfect the process, it has changed very little over time. The best coffees are roasted just prior to consumption, and most fall into one of the following broad categories:

- **Light Roasts:** delicate and mild; known as "cinnamon" roasts

- **Medium Roasts:** full-bodied, with light acidity; often called "city" or "full-city" roasts; the most popular breakfast coffee

- **Full Roasts:** dark, often bitter, oily beans; French, Italian, and Viennese roasts fall into this category

- **Double Roasts:** almost black and bitter; used in espresso and Turkish coffee.

FLAVORING COFFEE

Over the years, a variety of flavor enhancements have been added to or combined with coffee. Although coffee purists eschew flavored coffee beans, such specialty coffees have become increasingly popular in our country. Flavored whole-bean coffees—hazelnut and Irish creams, as well as chocolate, raspberry, cinnamon, and countless others—are readily available. Flavored coffees are generally made with beans that are roasted to a medium brown, then mixed with liquid flavoring agents. Although flavored coffees have a place in the coffee market, most coffee aficionados agree that liqueurs and syrups added after brewing provide better results than flavored beans.

Syrups made especially for flavoring coffee are available in many supermarkets, and are usually stocked in the coffee aisle, not to be confused with those in the ice cream toppings department. They come in a variety of flavors, including caramel, chocolate, and hazelnut. A small amount will add a distinctive accent to a cup of hot, brewed coffee.

BREWING

An estimated 1.5 billion cups of coffee are brewed daily around the world. The components of a great cup of coffee are simple: equipment, proportion, grind, water, and freshness.

Equipment

While it is entirely possible to brew a good cup of coffee with only rudimentary equipment, there are some excellent coffeemakers available today, all of which are designed to help you produce a better cup of java. The most popular are:

- **Automatic (Electric) Drip:** Most electric coffeepots made within the last decade fit this description. Water is poured into a well, where it is heated and then passed through finely ground coffee before dripping into a carafe. Automatic drip pots, which brew the coffee into a thermal carafe, are particularly practical since the carafe can be removed from the coffeemaker and will keep the coffee warm for a long period of time.

- **Filter Pots:** These pots are composed of two sections—a carafe, which is glass or ceramic, and a cone-shaped filter section. To brew coffee in a filter pot, you place a paper liner in the filter section, add finely ground coffee, and pour hot water slowly over the grinds. The water drips through the grinds to the carafe in only a few minutes.

- **The French Press:** Also known as a cafetière or plunger pot. This device, composed of a glass pitcher and a plunger, produces a rich brew easily. You simply place medium- to coarse-ground coffee in the bottom of the glass pot, pour hot water over the grinds, and allow them to steep for 3 to 5 minutes. Then you press the plunger to the bottom to separate the grounds from the brewed coffee, and pour.

- **Electric Espresso Machine:** There are a number of espresso machines available for the home kitchen. Each has a chamber for water and a filter section, which is filled with finely ground espresso coffee. Water is quickly forced by pressure through the filter holding the ground coffee to extract espresso, usually in 20 to 25 seconds. Another feature of these machines is a nozzle that froths milk. Newer espresso models offer the convenience of using small capsules prefilled with ground espresso. This method ensures that the exact amount of espresso is used. The capsule fits into a special slot in the machine, which is also equipped with a handle to eject the used pod.

- **Moka Espresso Pot:** Also called a stove-top espresso maker, this pot is a popular, inexpensive device for making espresso. Comprising three parts—a base chamber for water, a middle chamber for ground coffee, and a top chamber with a lid—it is easy to use. You fill the base with water, place finely ground coffee in the funnel or middle section, and screw on the top chamber. The pot is placed over medium heat on a stove top, and as the water in the base comes to a boil, it is pushed by pressure up through the coffee grinds, extracting their flavor, and finally arrives in the top chamber. This type of pot works best when the chamber for the coffee grinds is completely filled and so will produce several cups of espresso all at once.

- **Percolator:** Though many coffee fans believe that this machine should be consigned to a museum, it remains a fairly easy way to brew a large quantity of coffee. This old-fashioned device forces water up through a tube and into coarsely ground coffee. This weak first brew is forced back to the bottom and through the grounds again, gathering strength as it goes.

Proportion

Using the right proportion of ground coffee to water is essential when brewing coffee. For a flavorful cup of coffee, 1½ tablespoons ground coffee for each ⅔ cup of water is a good formula.

Grind

Use the grind best suited for the brewing method. As a general rule, the shorter the brewing process and the less time the grounds and water are in contact, the finer the grind you need. For instance, coffee ground for an espresso machine should be very fine, in part because of the very short brewing cycle. But, for a coffee press, the coffee should be medium to coarse grind, because the water and coffee are in direct contact for about four minutes.

Water

Use fresh, cold water heated to just below a boil (195 to 205 degrees F) in order to extract the coffee's full range of flavors. There are approximately 800 flavor compounds in coffee, with varying solubility temperatures, and those that taste the best are released by water just below a boil. Any cooler temperature, and the water can't do the job.

Freshness

Use freshly ground coffee. Store whole beans in an opaque, airtight container at room temperature. There is some proof that when coffee beans (in particular ground beans) are frozen, they absorb other odors in the freezer. Also, the oils of dark-roast beans tend to congeal when frozen, and some people believe that, once thawed, these beans never regain their full flavor.

FINISHING TOUCHES: MILK AND SUGAR

The most common ingredients added to coffee are milk or cream and sugar. Full-bodied coffees, brewed correctly, carry their flavor through nearly any reasonable amount of milk.

While you may simply drizzle a bit of refrigerated milk into your morning cup, nothing compares to the mixture of hot milk and hot coffee. Better still is the full, rich mouthfeel of properly steamed and foamed milk. With a home espresso machine or with one of the many milk steamers and frothers available in the marketplace today, you can produce steamed milk and foam to complement your coffee.

Coffee can be sweetened in a variety of ways, with syrups derived from fruit juice, pure cane sugar, and beet and corn sugars. Artificial sweeteners, like saccharine and aspartame, often tend to give off a flat, metallic flavor. By far the most common sweetener is plain table sugar.

TIPS AND HINTS

- Keep your coffeemaker clean following the manufacturer's directions.

- Use best-quality beans, and make certain they are the correct grind for your coffeemaker.

- When grinding your own beans (and this does result in exceptionally good coffee), brew the ground coffee immediately for the best results.

- If your tap water is not good quality, use bottled water.

- When using an automatic drip machine, you should count on making a minimum of two to three cups for best results.

- Automatic drip coffeemakers, which have thermal carafes, are preferable to those with glass ones that sit on a hot plate, sometimes scalding the coffee. If your coffeemaker has a glass carafe, you can transfer the brew to a thermos to prevent scalding.

- When using a filter coffeepot, the water should be heated to between 195 and 205 degrees F before it passes through the coffee.

- With most coffeemakers, and particularly with automatic drip machines, the amount of water you start with is reduced during the brewing process, since some is retained in the coffee grinds. Each coffeemaker will produce a slightly different yield.

- When frothing milk, start with cold milk—1 percent or 2 percent milk will foam best—and allow for expansion. Milk will double or triple in volume.

- Spices, sugar, and lemon and orange peels can be mixed in with ground coffee to add flavor and aroma.

- Whether you use filter paper or a gold filter in a coffeepot is a personal choice. A gold filter is practical since it can be cleaned and used repeatedly. Many coffee fans, however, believe that paper filters trap more impurities and yield a finer cup of coffee.

HOT
COFFEE DRINKS

AREN'T WE ALL CONVINCED THAT COFFEE CLEARS OUT

the cobwebs from our still-sleepy minds and gives us the kick to start another day?

In this chapter you'll find an array of hot coffee drinks to savor all through the day. You can wake up to The Perfect Cup of Coffee, an American-style brew ideal for sipping with breakfast, or indulge in Café au Lait, France's national morning coffee.

The Italian family of recipes made with espresso will brighten your mood whatever time you choose to sample them. A cup of thick hot Espresso, a Latte, a Cappuccino, a Macchiato, or a Caffè Moka are among the temptations.

Coffee pairs well with spirits, and you'll find some old-time favorites on the following pages, such as Irish Coffee and New Orleans Café Brûlot. Other novel creations include Anise Espresso and Sweet Dreams Nightcaps flavored with brandy.

Whatever type, wherever and whenever consumed, the hot coffee drinks in this chapter will serve, too, as social arbiters. To start a relationship, you might invite a potential sweetheart for a "cup of coffee"—definitely more impressive when you've brewed it yourself! If trying to close a business deal, you might suggest to the other party that you "discuss the details over *homemade* coffee." And, for that quintessential American custom—the coffee break at work—conversation will definitely be enhanced when the cups are filled with a delicious and freshly made brew.

Recipe yields in this chapter are for the amount of coffee and do not include toppings.

The Perfect Cup of Coffee

To make your cup of coffee, choose the type of bean and roast that you like. For a mild coffee flavor, choose a Colombian or a "house" blend, and for a stronger taste, use a French or Italian roast. The amount of ground coffee and water you use will determine how strong your brew turns out; 1 to 2 tablespoons ground coffee per ⅔ to 1 cup water falls within the traditional boundaries. Use the correct grind—coarse to fine—recommended for your coffeemaker.

6 tablespoons freshly ground coffee

2⅔ cups cold water

To brew the coffee, use a drip-style coffeepot (preferably an automatic drip coffeemaker), and line the filter cup with a paper or gold filter. Add the coffee, then pour the water into the water chamber. Brew according to the manufacturer's directions. Pour the coffee into warm cups.

MAKES FOUR 5-OUNCE SERVINGS

Caffè Macchiato

Macchiato means "marked," and for this espresso drink, hot espresso is poured into a demitasse cup, then marked with foam from steamed milk.

3 tablespoons milk

6 tablespoons freshly brewed espresso (see page 17)

If you have an espresso machine with a steamer and frothing (foaming) attachment, steam and froth the milk following the manufacturer's directions. Or, you can heat the milk and froth it using a manual frother following the manufacturer's directions. (Whichever way you steam and froth the milk, it will increase 2 or more times in volume.)

Pour half of the espresso into each of 2 warm demitasse cups. Top each serving with 1 to 2 teaspoons foam. Serve immediately.

MAKES TWO 1½-OUNCE SERVINGS (WITH A LITTLE MILK LEFTOVER)

Café au Lait

Café au lait (French for "coffee with milk") is prepared with strong, hot coffee and scalded milk. It is the national breakfast drink of France, where it is served steaming hot, often in large, wide bowls, to begin the day. The proportions can vary, with some versions calling for one part coffee and two parts milk, but I like to equalize the measures. Serve in warm coffee cups or in traditional French au lait bowls, as pictured on the facing page.

1½ cups whole milk

1½ cups extra-strength freshly brewed
  coffee (see Note)

Put the milk in a medium saucepan over medium heat. Heat until it is hot and small bubbles form around the edge of the pan. Remove the pan and add the hot coffee. Stir to mix. Pour the mixture into warm coffee cups.

MAKES FOUR 6-OUNCE SERVINGS

Note:
I use ¾ cup dark-roasted ground coffee to 2 cups water to yield about 1½ cups extra-strength brewed coffee.

Espresso

Espresso is Italian for "fast," and this quintessential Italian coffee drink doesn't take long for home cooks to produce.

¾ cup cold water

¼ cup finely ground Italian or French espresso coffee

4 lemon strips (optional)

Prepare the espresso in an espresso machine or in a moka espresso pot according to the manufacturer's directions. Serve the espresso in 4 warm demitasse cups, filling each about half full. If desired, garnish each cup with a lemon strip.

MAKES FOUR 1½-OUNCE SERVINGS

Latte

Caffè latte is Italian for "coffee with milk"—Italy's version of the French café au lait. A single serving is traditionally made with 3 tablespoons (1½ ounces) freshly brewed espresso and ½ to ¾ cup (4 to 6 ounces) steamed milk. The following recipe yields four lattes, but can be halved easily.

2 cups milk

¾ cup freshly brewed espresso (see above)

If you have an espresso machine, steam the milk using the steaming attachment, following the manufacturer's directions. Otherwise, you can simply heat the milk in a saucepan over high heat until it is scalded (when small bubbles form around the edge of the pan).

Fill a warm, standard-size (5- to 6-ounce) coffee cup with 3 tablespoons espresso, then add ½ cup steamed milk. Repeat to make 3 more servings. Serve immediately.

MAKES FOUR 5½-OUNCE SERVINGS

Cappuccino

Many fans proclaim that cappuccino is a celestial brew and might not be surprised to learn that its name has a religious connection. The word *cappuccino* is associated with the brown and white cowl worn by Capuchin monks in Italy. A traditional cappuccino is made with one part espresso, one part steamed milk, and one part foam. A dusting of cinnamon or some shaved chocolate are popular garnishes. I generally brew the espresso first, then steam and froth the milk.

⅔ cup milk, preferably nonfat or 1 percent

⅔ cup freshly brewed espresso (see page 17)

Cinnamon or shaved chocolate for garnish (optional)

If you have an espresso machine with a steamer and frothing (foaming) attachment, steam and froth the milk following the manufacturer's directions. Or, you can heat the milk and froth it using a manual frother following the manufacturer's directions. (Whichever way you steam and froth the milk, it will increase 2 or more times in volume.)

Fill 2 warm, standard-size coffee cups each with ⅓ cup espresso, then with ⅓ cup steamed milk. Top each with ⅓ cup foam. Dust with cinnamon or sprinkle with shaved chocolate, if desired.

MAKES TWO 5- TO 6-OUNCE SERVINGS

Caffè Moka

Made with espresso and a touch of chocolate syrup, caffè moka is a good example of that timeless flavor combination—coffee and chocolate. The two strong tastes complement each other beautifully in this recipe.

½ cup milk

4 teaspoons chocolate syrup (see Note)

6 tablespoons freshly brewed espresso (see page 17)

2 tablespoons softly whipped cream, unsweetened (optional)

Cocoa powder for garnish (optional)

If you have an espresso machine with a steamer attachment, steam the milk following the manufacturer's directions. (The milk will not increase in volume.) Otherwise, you can simply heat the milk in a saucepan over high heat until scalded (when small bubbles form around the edge of the pan).

Spoon 2 teaspoons of the syrup into each of 2 warm, standard-size coffee cups. Pour half of the espresso into each, top with some steamed milk, and, if desired, a dollop of whipped cream. Lightly dust with cocoa powder if you wish.

MAKES TWO 4-OUNCE SERVINGS

Note:

Flavored syrups specifically made to use with coffee are sold in some supermarkets, usually in the same aisle with the coffees, and also in some coffee cafés. These syrups are strong and intense, and should not be replaced with dessert syrups found in the ice cream toppings aisle of your supermarket. Monin and Torani are two well-known brands. Since the flavor and intensity of the syrup can vary with the brand used, feel free to adjust according to your own taste.

Holiday Spiced Coffee with Brandied Whipped Cream

Stirring fragrant spices—cardamom, cinnamon, and nutmeg—into ground coffee before brewing it produces an enticing beverage with an alluring aroma and a seductive flavor. Dollops of brandy-scented whipped cream mounded atop cups of this spiced brew make a decadent garnish. Add a minute sprinkling of ground spices if you wish! Although this special coffee is good any day of the year, I love to serve it during the holidays as a memorable finale to a Christmas or New Year's brunch.

¾ cup heavy or whipping cream

1½ tablespoons confectioners' sugar

1 tablespoon brandy

⅓ cup freshly ground coffee, preferably a mild roast such as Colombian (see Note)

2½ teaspoons ground cardamom

1½ teaspoons sugar

1 teaspoon ground cinnamon

½ teaspoon freshly grated nutmeg

5½ cups cold water

With an electric mixer on medium-high speed, beat the cream in a medium bowl until it starts to mound softly, then beat in the confectioners' sugar and brandy. Continue beating until it is just firm. If not using it right away, cover the bowl of whipped cream with plastic wrap and refrigerate it. (The whipped cream can be prepared 1 day ahead.)

To brew the coffee, use a drip-style coffeepot (preferably an automatic drip coffeemaker) and line the filter cup with a paper filter. Put the coffee, cardamom, sugar, cinnamon, and nutmeg in the filter. Mix gently with a spoon to combine the spices with the coffee. Add the water to the water chamber, and brew according to the manufacturer's directions.

To serve, pour the coffee into 8 warm cups and garnish each cup with a generous dollop of the whipped cream. The cream will melt as it floats on top. Serve immediately.

MAKES EIGHT 5½-OUNCE SERVINGS

Note:
Dark-roast coffee doesn't work as well with the spices in this recipe. Colombian or another mild coffee works best.

Irish Coffee

The story goes that Irish coffee was created in the mid-twentieth century in the Shannon airport in Ireland, where it was a restorative drink served to weary passengers. The recipe is said to have been brought back to the States by a San Franciscan who shared it with the Buena Vista Bar in his hometown. The hot, strong coffee infused with Irish whiskey became the signature drink of the California bar, and eventually its popularity spread throughout our country. Today, Irish coffee is popular around the globe. The following version is my favorite.

4 tablespoons good-quality Irish whiskey (Jameson's works well)

8 teaspoons sugar

1⅓ cups freshly brewed coffee, preferably strong French roast

½ cup heavy or whipping cream, whipped to soft peaks

Place 1 tablespoon whiskey and 2 teaspoons sugar in each of 4 warm Irish coffee or 8-ounce heat-proof glasses. Stir with a spoon until the sugar dissolves. Pour enough hot coffee into each glass to fill it about three-quarters full.

Hold a tablespoon (with the back of the spoon facing you) over the coffee in one cup, and ladle 2 to 3 tablespoons of the whipped cream over the spoon so that it gently falls into the coffee. Adding the cream this way will help it float on top of the coffee instead of sinking immediately to the bottom. Repeat to make 3 more servings. Serve immediately.

MAKES FOUR 3½-OUNCE SERVINGS

Sweet Dreams Nightcaps

For this recipe, I follow the directions for The Perfect Cup of Coffee, but add some coarsely chopped cinnamon sticks to the coffee grinds for an aromatic accent. After pouring the coffee into cups, I splash each serving with some brandy and top with a dollop of White Chocolate Whipped Cream.

1 recipe The Perfect Cup of Coffee
  (page 13)

Two 2- to 3-inch cinnamon sticks,
  coarsely chopped

4 tablespoons brandy

1 recipe White Chocolate Whipped
  Cream (page 73)

Ground cinnamon for garnish

Prepare The Perfect Cup of Coffee recipe, adding the cinnamon sticks to the ground coffee before brewing.

Divide the coffee among 4 standard-size (5- to 6-ounce) coffee cups, and stir 1 tablespoon of brandy into each. Top each serving with one quarter of the whipped cream and sprinkle it with cinnamon.

MAKES FOUR 5- TO 6-OUNCE SERVINGS

Anise Espresso

A touch of Pernod provides an unexpected and pleasant accent to a cup of steaming hot espresso.

½ teaspoon Pernod, plus more if needed

2 tablespoons finely ground Italian
  or French espresso

½ teaspoon chopped lemon peel, plus
  2 lemon strips for garnish

6 tablespoons cold water

Pour ¼ teaspoon Pernod into each of 2 warm demitasse cups.

Put the coffee and chopped peel in a small bowl and stir to blend. Brew the mixture with the water in an espresso machine or a moka espresso pot according to the manufacturer's directions.

Add a lemon strip to each of the demitasse cups. Pour in the hot espresso. For a stronger anise accent, add a drop or two more of Pernod to each cup.

MAKES TWO 1½-OUNCE SERVINGS

New Orleans Café Brûlot

New Orleans is well-known for Café Brûlot—hot brewed coffee combined with flamed brandy, sugar, spices, and orange and lemon slices. This warm spiced brew is then poured into demitasse cups. The word *brûlot* derives from the French word *brûler,* which means "to burn."

3 thin orange slices, quartered

3 thin lemon slices, quartered

¼ cup sugar

Two 3-inch cinnamon sticks, coarsely chopped

20 cloves

2 cups freshly brewed coffee

¼ cup brandy

Have ready 6 warm demitasse cups and saucers.

Put the orange and lemon slices, sugar, cinnamon, and cloves in a medium, nonreactive saucepan. Add the coffee and set the pan over very low heat, just to keep the coffee warm while you flame the brandy.

Put the brandy in a small saucepan and set it over medium-high heat. When the brandy just starts to boil, avert your face, and flame the brandy with a lit match (preferably a wooden match). Turn off the heat, and when the flame in the brandy goes out after a few seconds, add the brandy to the coffee.

To serve, ladle the coffee, with spices and citrus slices, into the demitasse cups.

MAKES SIX 4- TO 5-OUNCE SERVINGS

COLD
COFFEE DRINKS

THE COLD COFFEE DRINKS INCLUDED HERE ARE JUST AS

seductive as their hot counterparts. They are guaranteed to refresh your palate, restore your spirit, and encourage conversation. Classic iced coffee made with freshly brewed (or even leftover) coffee is the perfect answer to a heat wave, but there are countless variations on the original. Try, for example, Chilled Cappuccinos Topped with Mascarpone Whipped Cream (made with a base of espresso) or Vietnamese Iced Coffee, a combination of a dark, strong brew and sweetened condensed milk. Aromatic spices add a distinctive accent to Chilled Chai Coffee, while a splash of rum provides a rich note for Coffee–Rum Smoothies.

Besides iced coffee, there are other tempting cold drinks in which coffee plays a starring role. In this chapter, for example, you'll find Old-Fashioned Coffee Sodas, eggnog assembled with a coffee-scented custard, and coffee milkshakes.

Coffee-scented drinks that include shots of liquor provide an extra jolt! For my version of a Black Russian, vodka, coffee liqueur, and brewed coffee are the essential ingredients. The Black Russian becomes a White Russian with the addition of a little cream. For a hip new coffee drink, there's an Espresso Martini—an absolutely delicious concoction made with chilled espresso, vodka, Kahlúa, crème de cacao, and half-and-half.

As mentioned for hot drinks, the recipe yields in this chapter are for the amount of coffee and do not include toppings.

Classic Iced Coffee

The perfect respite on a hot day is a glass of icy-cold coffee. Nothing is simpler to prepare, but a few guidelines will ensure that your chilled brew is the best ever. First, use strong brewed coffee because as the ice melts, it dilutes the mixture. Second, even though ice cubes work fine, crushed ice chills the coffee even quicker. And, finally, even if you always drink hot coffee black, try swirling a little half-and-half or cream into your iced java. The velvety smoothness of cream enhances a cold brew immeasurably. Whether you sweeten your iced coffee is an individual matter, but since the coffee is strong, a touch of sugar is usually a welcome addition.

½ cup freshly ground coffee (such as Colombian or a house blend)

2⅔ cups cold water

Coarsely crushed ice

4 tablespoons half-and-half or light cream

Sugar for serving (optional)

To brew the coffee, use a drip-style coffeepot (preferably an automatic drip coffeemaker) and line the filter cup with a paper or gold filter. Add the ground coffee, then pour the water into the water chamber. Brew according to the manufacturer's directions.

Pour the brewed coffee into a medium heat-proof bowl and refrigerate it until chilled.

Fill 4 medium glasses with ice, and divide the coffee evenly among them. Stir 1 tablespoon half-and-half into each glass. Allow each person to sweeten his or her coffee with sugar to taste, if desired.

MAKES FOUR 5- TO 6-OUNCE SERVINGS

Note:
If you are in a hurry, put the bowl of coffee in the freezer and put a small self-sealing plastic bag filled with ice cubes in the container of coffee. It will take only a few minutes for the coffee to chill this way.

Vietnamese Iced Coffee

For those who like their coffee strong with a good hint of sweetness, Vietnamese coffee, made with dark, rich robust beans and condensed milk, will be satisfying.

¾ cup chilled brewed espresso
  (see page 17)

¼ cup sweetened condensed milk

Coarsely crushed ice

In a measuring cup with a spout, stir together the coffee and milk. Fill 2 medium wineglasses or other decorative glasses two-thirds full with ice. Pour half of the coffee mixture into each glass and serve immediately.

MAKES TWO 4-OUNCE SERVINGS

Mocha Madness

The recipe for this delectable chilled coffee drink came to me from my friend Tom Johnson. When he was a chef at Shaw's Restaurant in Lancaster, Ohio, this was a frequent bar request.

⅔ cup best-quality vanilla ice cream

¼ cup chilled brewed coffee
  (see Note, page 29)

3 tablespoons dark crème de cacao

3 tablespoons Kahlúa or other
  coffee liqueur

Coarsely crushed ice

Put the ice cream, coffee, crème de cacao, and Kahlúa in a blender. Blend until smooth. Fill 2 medium wineglasses or two 8-ounce brandy snifters with ice. Divide the mixture evenly between the 2 glasses. Serve immediately.

MAKES TWO 5-OUNCE SERVINGS

Coffee Eggnog

Eggnog is the quintessential holiday drink, and in this version, the original gets an update with the addition of coffee. The creamy coffee-scented custard base of the eggnog can be prepared several hours ahead, and the egg whites whipped and added at serving time. Although the following recipe serves six, it can be doubled or tripled as needed.

4 large eggs, separated (see Note)	1 tablespoon powdered instant coffee
2 cups whole milk	6 tablespoons cognac or other brandy
½ cup sugar	Ground nutmeg for sprinkling (optional)

Put the egg yolks in a medium, heavy saucepan, and add the milk and sugar. Place the pan over medium-low heat, and whisk constantly until the sugar has dissolved, about 1 minute. Add the coffee, and continue to whisk until the mixture thickens and coats the back of a spoon, 4 to 5 minutes.

Remove the pan from the heat and stir in the cognac. Transfer the mixture to a large bowl and refrigerate until it is cold, 1 hour or longer.

With an electric mixer on high speed, beat the egg whites in a medium bowl just until soft peaks form. Gently fold the whites into the eggnog mixture. Serve the eggnog in clear glass mugs or medium glasses or, if you are lucky enough to have them, in silver mint julep cups. Sprinkle with ground nutmeg if desired.

MAKES SIX 4½- TO 5-OUNCE SERVINGS

Note:
The egg whites in this recipe are uncooked. Food safety experts caution that consuming raw egg whites (or yolks) can expose you to salmonella contamination. Immuno-compromised patients, the very young, and the elderly should not eat raw eggs.

Old-Fashioned Coffee Sodas

Drugstores with soda fountain counters might be a thing of the past, but ice cream sodas will never go out of style. Good-quality ice cream, a little soda water, a flavoring of your choice, and some whipped cream are all you need to make this timeless favorite. For this version, I combine coffee ice cream with brewed and chilled coffee for a big java burst. A touch of fizzy soda and a garnish of softly whipped cream make these sodas irresistible. I sometimes gild the lily by adding a drop of coffee liqueur to the mix.

3 cups chilled brewed coffee, preferably made from a mild Colombian
  or house blend (see Note, page 29)

1½ tablespoons sugar

3 cups (1½ pints) coffee ice cream,
  either homemade (page 77) or
  good-quality purchased

1 cup soda water

4 teaspoons Kahlúa or other coffee
  liqueur (optional)

½ cup heavy or whipping cream,
  whipped to soft peaks

Shaved dark chocolate (optional)

Pour the coffee into a 4-cup or larger glass measuring cup with a spout, and stir in the sugar.

Place 2 large scoops (about ⅓ cup each) ice cream into each of 4 tall glasses. Pour ¾ cup sweetened coffee into each glass, then add ¼ cup soda water to each. If desired, add 1 teaspoon Kahlúa to each serving. Top the sodas with some whipped cream and, if desired, sprinkle them with shaved chocolate. Serve with straws and long spoons.

MAKES FOUR 13-OUNCE SERVINGS

The 3 "Cs" Milkshakes

A trinity of delectable flavors—chocolate, caramel, and coffee—are the three "Cs" referred to in this recipe title. All that is necessary to prepare these special shakes is to whirl together coffee ice cream, caramel and chocolate syrups, and a little milk in a blender or food processor. Serve the milkshakes in tall glasses with straws.

2 cups (1 pint) best-quality coffee
ice cream (see page 77)

2 tablespoons whole milk

2 tablespoons each caramel and
chocolate syrup (see Note)

Put the ice cream, milk, and syrups in a blender or food processor, and blend or process several seconds until smooth.

Divide the mixture between 2 tall glasses and serve with straws.

MAKES TWO 9- TO 10-OUNCE SERVINGS

Note:

Flavored syrups specifically made to use with coffee are sold in some super-markets, usually in the same aisle with the coffees, and also in some coffee cafés. These syrups are strong and intense, and should not be replaced with dessert syrups found in the ice cream toppings aisle. Monin and Torani are two well-known brands. Since the flavor and intensity of the syrup can vary with the brand used, feel free to adjust according to your own taste.

Black Russian with Coffee

Traditionally, Black Russians are two parts vodka to one part coffee liqueur served over a glassful of ice. This recipe features an additional shot of coffee, which intensifies the coffee flavor.

Coarsely crushed ice

¼ cup vodka

2 tablespoons Kahlúa or other coffee liqueur

3 to 4 tablespoons chilled or room temperature brewed coffee (see Note, page 29)

Fill a short 8- to 10-ounce old-fashioned glass with ice. Pour the vodka and Kahlúa over the ice and stir. Add 3 tablespoons coffee to the glass, and stir. Taste and, if you prefer a stronger coffee flavor, stir in the additional tablespoon of coffee.

MAKES ONE 4½-OUNCE SERVING

White Russian with Coffee

The White Russian is a Black Russian that is splashed with heavy cream. It is slightly sweeter and more mellow than the original.

Coarsely crushed ice

¼ cup vodka

2 tablespoons Kahlúa or other coffee liqueur

3 to 4 tablespoons chilled or room temperature brewed coffee (see Note, page 29)

1 tablespoon heavy or whipping cream

Fill a short 8- to10-ounce old-fashioned glass with ice. Pour the vodka and Kahlúa over the ice and stir. Add 3 tablespoons coffee to the glass and stir. Taste and, if you prefer a stronger coffee flavor, stir in the additional tablespoon of coffee. Add the cream and swirl or stir to blend.

MAKES ONE 5-OUNCE SERVING

Espresso Martini

Peter Brown, the twenty-something son of my assistant, Deb Brown, from Amherst, Massachusetts, created this unusual and enticing martini.

Coarsely crushed ice

¼ cup chilled or room temperature brewed espresso (see page 17)

¼ cup vodka

2 tablespoons Kahlúa or other coffee liqueur

2 tablespoons dark crème de cacao

2 tablespoons half-and-half

1 or 2 coffee beans (real beans, not chocolate-coated coffee bean candies)

Fill a martini shaker or a large glass jar with a lid with ice. Pour the espresso, vodka, Kahlúa, crème de cacao, and half-and-half over the ice. Cover the shaker or jar, and shake vigorously. Strain the liquid into a chilled martini glass. Spoon any froth remaining in the shaker on top of the martini. Float 1 or 2 coffee beans in the froth as a garnish. Remove the beans before drinking.

MAKES ONE 7-OUNCE SERVING

Coffee–Rum Smoothies

When you have leftover coffee, try using it to make these decadently rich and satisfying smoothies.

1 tablespoon packed light brown sugar

¾ cup chilled or room temperature brewed coffee (see Note, page 29)

1 cup (½ pint) best-quality vanilla ice cream

2 tablespoons dark rum

Coarsely crushed ice

In a small bowl, stir the sugar into the coffee until the sugar dissolves. Put the coffee mixture, ice cream, and rum in a blender or food processor and process until the mixture is smooth and creamy, only a few seconds. Fill two 10-ounce glasses half full with ice, and pour half of the coffee mixture into each.

MAKES TWO 7½-OUNCE SERVINGS

Chilled Chai Coffee

Editor Kim Upton shared this delectable chai recipe with me. In place of tea leaves, ground coffee is steeped with an aromatic spice mixture. Then milk and sweeteners, including both honey and sugar, are added. Chai drinks like this one are typically served hot, but are just as tempting when chilled.

3 cups cold water

5 nickel-sized thin slices peeled fresh
  ginger

12 cloves

One 3- to 4-inch cinnamon stick, broken in half, plus 4 for garnish
  (optional)

1 teaspoon anise seeds

¼ teaspoon ground cardamom

2 tablespoons finely ground coffee
  such as Colombian (not powdered
  instant coffee)

1 cup whole milk

2 to 3 tablespoons sugar

2 to 3 tablespoons honey

Coarsely crushed ice

Put the water, ginger, cloves, broken cinnamon stick, anise, and cardamom in a medium saucepan set over medium-high heat. Bring to a boil, then reduce the heat and simmer 15 minutes.

Remove the pan from the heat and stir in the coffee grinds. Let them steep 5 minutes.

Line a fine-mesh sieve with a double thickness of paper towels and set it over a 2-cup or larger measuring cup with a spout. Pour the steeped coffee through the sieve to remove the spices and grounds. Rinse the saucepan to remove any grounds left in the pan and wipe it dry. Return the strained coffee to the saucepan and stir in the milk and 2 tablespoons each of sugar and honey. (For a sweeter drink, use an extra tablespoon each of sugar and honey; the sugar and honey should be used in equal proportions.)

Set the saucepan over medium-high heat and bring the coffee just to a boil, then remove it from the heat. Pour the coffee back into the measuring cup and chill (see Note, page 29).

To serve, fill 4 large wineglasses with ice, and divide the chilled coffee among them. Garnish each with a cinnamon stick, if desired.

MAKES FOUR 8-OUNCE SERVINGS

Chilled Cappuccinos Topped with Mascarpone Whipped Cream

In this cold version of one of the world's most popular coffees, chilled espresso is combined with milk and poured into ice-filled glasses. Clouds of cream whipped with mascarpone and sweetened with a touch of vanilla and sugar top these iced coffees.

MASCARPONE WHIPPED CREAM
1 cup heavy or whipping cream

6 tablespoons mascarpone cheese

2 tablespoons sugar

½ teaspoon vanilla extract

Coarsely crushed ice

¾ cup chilled brewed espresso
 (see page 17)

¾ cup whole milk

Ground cinnamon for garnish (optional)

To make the Mascarpone Whipped Cream: With an electric mixer on medium-high speed, whip the cream in a medium bowl until it just starts to thicken, then add the mascarpone and sugar. Continue beating until the cream is just firm. Stir in the vanilla. (The mascarpone cream can be made 3 hours ahead. Cover and refrigerate it.) Makes about 2 cups.

To make the cappuccinos: Fill 2 tall 12-ounce glasses with ice. Combine the coffee and milk in a pitcher or in a 2-cup or larger measuring cup with a spout. Divide the liquid between the 2 glasses and scoop ½ cup Mascarpone Whipped Cream on top of each. (You will have some mascarpone whipped cream left over. Refrigerate and save it for another use.) Dust the tops with cinnamon, if desired.

MAKES TWO 6-OUNCE SERVINGS

SWEET TREATS
FOR DIPPING OR NIBBLING
WITH COFFEE

COFFEE AND SUGAR ARE NATURAL PARTNERS, SO IT'S

no wonder that we like to nibble on something sweet when sipping on a cup of java. All of the confections in this chapter are baked, and include cookies and cakes, a luscious tart, and some pastry twists and cups. Coffee (often in the form of powdered instant) flavors many, but not all, of these sweets. Chocolate, orange, cinnamon, cardamom, ginger, and a trio of nuts—pecans, walnuts, and hazelnuts—all complement coffee, and you'll find them used generously in the following recipes.

If you like to dip cookies in your coffee, you're in luck. Butter-rich Hazelnut Stars, Pecan Shortbreads, or Cappuccino Icebox Cookies will make you smile with each coffee-drenched bite. For extra crunchiness, try the Ginger–Cherry Biscotti or the Walnut Meringue Cookies.

For those who consider coffee and chocolate a celestial union (and I am one of them), you'll want to sample the Chocolate–Cream Cheese Brownies, the Irish Coffee–Chocolate Tart, and the Chocolate-Pecan Phyllo Cups with Coffee Whipped Cream.

Ginger Twists—twirled puff pastry sticks studded with bits of crystallized ginger—make distinctive nibbles to set beside a cup of espresso or latte.

And, if you are hosting a coffee and dessert party, the tall, stately Light as Air Cake with Coffee-Toffee Icing, which easily serves twelve, is a perfect choice to offer with hot or iced coffees.

Cappuccino Icebox Cookies

These thin, crisp coffee-scented cookies are baked until they turn a rich cappuccino brown. After the dough is shaped into a roll, it is put in the freezer for a few minutes to firm before slices are cut from it and baked. You can keep a roll of this dough in the freezer for several weeks and use it as needed.

¼ teaspoon powdered instant coffee

1 teaspoon vanilla extract

8 tablespoons (1 stick) unsalted
   butter, at room temperature

½ cup granulated sugar

½ cup packed brown sugar

1 teaspoon ground cinnamon

1 large egg

1½ cups all-purpose flour, sifted

¼ cup slivered almonds

In a small bowl, dissolve the coffee in the vanilla and set aside.

With an electric mixer on medium-high speed, cream the butter in a large bowl until smooth, 1 minute or more. Add the sugars and cinnamon. Beat well to incorporate them, about 3 minutes. Add the egg and beat until it is blended. Then beat in the coffee and vanilla mixture. Reduce the speed to low, and add the flour. Beat, stopping the machine and scraping down the sides of the bowl with a spatula if needed, only until the mixture is smooth and holds together, about one minute or less.

Place the dough on a long piece of waxed paper. Shape it into a long roll about 2 inches wide and 10 inches long. (The dough will be quite sticky at this point.) Use the waxed paper to wrap the dough. Place the roll in the freezer until the dough is stiff and firm, about 25 minutes. (If you want to freeze the dough, wrap it in plastic wrap rather than waxed paper, then tightly in foil. The dough can be frozen for 1 month; when ready to use, remove and defrost it overnight in the refrigerator.)

Preheat the oven to 350 degrees F. Adjust 2 oven racks to divide the oven into thirds.

Unwrap the dough and with a sharp knife, cut it into ¼- to ⅜-inch-thick slices. Place the slices 1 inch apart on 2 ungreased baking sheets. Place a slivered almond in the center of each cookie. Bake until the cookies are lightly colored, 18 to 20 minutes. Reverse the baking sheets, top to bottom and back to front, once during the cooking time. Be careful not to underbake these cookies, as they should be very crisp when cooled. Remove and cool the cookies on a cooling rack.

MAKES 24 TO 30 COOKIES

Hazelnut Stars

The dough for these butter-rich nut cookies is prepared in a food processor and takes only a few seconds to assemble. I like to use a star-shaped cutter to cut cookies from the rolled-out dough, but a round one works equally well. You can serve these shortbreads unadorned or embellish them with a drizzle of melted white chocolate.

2 cups all-purpose flour, plus extra for dusting work surface

½ cup sugar

⅓ cup cornstarch

1 cup (2 sticks) unsalted butter, chilled and cut into small pieces

½ teaspoon vanilla extract

1 generous cup hazelnuts, toasted for 8 minutes in a 350°F oven, skins rubbed off, and nuts coarsely chopped

4 ounces white chocolate, melted (optional)

Arrange an oven rack at center position and preheat the oven to 350 degrees F. Have ready a large, ungreased baking sheet.

Put the flour, sugar, and cornstarch in a food processor fitted with the metal blade. Add the butter and vanilla, then process, pulsing several times, until the mixture is crumbly. Add the hazelnuts and process until the mixture is combined but remains slightly crumbly.

Place the dough on a lightly floured work surface and shape it into a ball. Knead until it is smooth. Divide the dough in half; wrap each half in plastic wrap, and chill until it is firm enough to handle, about 30 minutes.

Roll half the dough at a time on a lightly floured work surface until it is ¼ to ½ inch thick. Cut the dough into stars or rounds with a 2½- to 3-inch cookie cutter. Reshape and roll out the dough again and cut out more cookies. Continue until all the dough is used. Place the cutouts 1 inch apart on the ungreased baking sheet. Pierce each cutout 3 times with a fork, going all the way through to the baking sheet.

Bake until the edges and bottoms of the cookies just start to brown, about 15 minutes. Transfer them to a wire rack to cool. If desired, drizzle the cooled cookies in a zigzag pattern with the melted white chocolate. (The cookies can be prepared 2 days ahead; store them in an airtight container at room temperature.)

MAKES ABOUT 30 COOKIES

Ginger–Cherry Biscotti

Italy's most famous cookies are biscotti, whose name translates as "twice baked." The cookie dough is shaped into logs and baked once until it is light golden. Then the logs are cut into slices, which are returned to the oven and baked again until they are crisp and light brown. The following biscotti, dotted with crimson-hued dried cherries and flavored with orange and ginger, make a delectable accompaniment to dip in a cup of your favorite coffee.

½ cup dried cherries

⅔ cup freshly squeezed orange juice

4 tablespoons (½ stick) unsalted
  butter, at room temperature

¾ cup sugar

½ teaspoon baking powder

2 large eggs

4 teaspoons grated orange zest

2¼ cups all-purpose flour

⅓ cup chopped crystallized ginger

Arrange an oven rack at center position and preheat the oven to 350 degrees F.

Put the cherries in a small bowl. Heat the orange juice in a small saucepan over medium heat until it is warm; pour it over the cherries and let them stand until they are soft, 10 to 15 minutes. Drain well, pressing the cherries to remove any excess liquid. Discard the juice and set the cherries aside.

With an electric mixer on medium speed, beat the butter in a large bowl for 30 seconds. Add the sugar and baking powder, and beat until they are combined, about 1 minute. Beat in the eggs and zest. Then beat in the flour, until it is just combined. Stir in the cherries and ginger with a wooden spoon.

Divide the dough into 3 portions. With lightly floured hands, shape each portion into a 9-by-2-inch log; place the logs 3 inches apart on an ungreased baking sheet. Bake until the tops are lightly browned, about 25 minutes. Set the baking sheet with biscotti on a wire rack to cool for 20 minutes. Reduce the oven temperature to 300 degrees F.

With a serrated knife, cut each roll diagonally into ½-inch-thick slices. Place the slices upright on the baking sheet, leaving ½ inch between them. Bake again until the biscotti are crisp and golden, 15 to 20 minutes. Transfer the cookies to wire racks and cool. Store them up to 1 week in an airtight container at room temperature.

MAKES ABOUT 40 BISCOTTI

Walnut Meringue Cookies

One fall, while teaching in southwestern France, I bought some beautiful walnut meringues in an outdoor market in the town of Sarlat. I was dazzled by the assertive taste of ground walnuts that had been baked into the crispy, golden rounds. I ate the cookies several days in a row, trying to figure out, with each bite, how they were made. I hope you enjoy the result!

Butter for greasing baking sheets

1½ cups walnut halves or pieces

¾ cup confectioners' sugar

1 tablespoon all-purpose flour

3 large egg whites

6 tablespoons granulated sugar

1 cup bittersweet chocolate chips such as Ghirardelli's "Double Chocolate"

Line 2 baking sheets with aluminum foil and butter the foil generously. Position oven racks at the lower and center positions, and preheat the oven to 300 degrees F.

Process the walnuts in a food processor or blender until they are finely ground. Put them in a medium bowl. Sift the confectioners' sugar and flour together over the nuts. Mix them well with a spoon.

Put the egg whites and granulated sugar in the bowl of an electric mixer and beat them on medium-high speed until soft peaks form, 4 to 5 minutes. Remove the bowl and fold in half the walnut mixture. Then fold in the remaining walnut mixture along with the chocolate.

Using a tablespoon, scoop a generous amount of batter onto a prepared baking sheet. Use a table knife to help release the meringue batter from the spoon. Lightly flatten the top of the meringue with the blade of the knife. Continue until all the batter has been used, leaving at least 1 inch around each meringue.

Bake until the meringues are light golden brown and crisp, about 25 minutes. Reverse the baking sheets top to bottom after 10 minutes.

Remove the baking sheets from the oven and cool the cookies on them, 15 minutes or longer. Then gently peel the meringues from the foil. Store them in an airtight container at room temperature for up to 1 week.

MAKES 30 TO 32 COOKIES

Pecan Shortbreads

These cookies are similar to the Hazelnut Stars on page 47 and take little time to make because the dough is assembled in a food processor. The generous amount of butter, plus the chopped pecans, in these little confections make them irresistibly rich and moist. A single recipe yields sixteen cookies, but the ingredients can be doubled easily. Serve these cookies with a bowl of fresh berries and iced coffee in warm weather or with ripe pears and cups of hot coffee in the winter months.

1 cup all-purpose flour, plus extra for dusting work surface

¼ cup sugar

2½ tablespoons cornstarch

8 tablespoons (1 stick) unsalted butter, chilled and cut into small pieces, plus extra for greasing baking sheet

½ teaspoon vanilla extract

½ cup pecans, toasted for 5 to 6 minutes in a 350°F oven, and nuts coarsely chopped

Put the flour, sugar, and cornstarch in the bowl of a food processor fitted with the metal blade. Add the butter and vanilla and process, pulsing several times, until the mixture is crumbly. Add the pecans and process until the mixture resembles a crumbly mass, about 20 seconds. The mixture should not form a ball of dough.

Place the dough on a lightly floured work surface and knead it several times until it is smooth. Divide the dough into 3 equal pieces. Using the heel of your hand, press down on one of the pieces of dough and smear it into a thin sheet on the work surface. This technique will ensure that the flour and fat are well blended. Repeat with the remaining pieces of dough. Then gather all the dough into a ball, knead it a time or two, and flatten it into a disk. Cover it with plastic wrap and refrigerate it for 30 minutes.

Arrange an oven rack at center position and preheat the oven to 375 degrees F. Butter a baking sheet and set aside.

Place a large sheet of waxed paper on a work surface and flour it lightly. Place the dough in the center and cover it with another large sheet of waxed paper. Roll the dough into a circle ¼ to ⅜ inch thick. Remove the top layer of waxed paper and, using a 2-inch fluted or plain cookie cutter, cut out as

(continued)

many rounds as you can and transfer them to the prepared baking sheet. Reshape and, replacing the top layer of waxed paper, roll out the dough again and cut out more cookies. Continue until all the dough is used. You should get 16 cookies.

Cover the cookies on the baking sheet with plastic wrap and refrigerate them until they are firm, 10 to 15 minutes. Remove the plastic and bake the cookies until they are lightly browned on the bottom and top, 15 to 18 minutes. Transfer the cookies to a cooling rack to cool completely. (The cookies can be baked 2 days ahead; store them in an airtight container at room tmperature.)

MAKES 16 COOKIES

Chocolate–Cream Cheese Brownies

These brownies are moist, dense, and intensely chocolate flavored. Cream cheese added to the batter provides a subtle creamy note, while chopped walnuts contribute crunchiness to the texture. Iced with a rich, coffee-scented chocolate glaze, these sweet confections can be made several days ahead and stored in the refrigerator.

5 tablespoons (⅔ stick) unsalted butter, divided, plus extra for greasing baking pan

4 ounces semisweet chocolate, coarsely chopped

3 ounces cream cheese

1 cup sugar, divided

3 large eggs, divided

½ cup plus 1 tablespoon all-purpose flour, divided, plus extra for flouring baking pan

1½ teaspoons vanilla extract, divided

½ teaspoon baking powder

¼ teaspoon salt

½ cup coarsely chopped walnuts

ICING
6 ounces semisweet chocolate, coarsely chopped

½ cup heavy or whipping cream

1½ teaspoons powdered instant coffee

Arrange an oven rack at center position and preheat the oven to 350 degrees F. Generously butter an 8-inch square baking pan and dust it with flour. Shake out the excess flour and set the pan aside.

Melt 3 tablespoons of the butter and the chocolate in a heavy, medium saucepan over very low heat, stirring constantly until the mixture is smooth and creamy. Remove the pan from the heat and cool it slightly.

With an electric mixer on medium speed, cream the remaining 2 tablespoons of butter with the cream cheese in a medium bowl. Gradually add ¼ cup of the sugar and beat until it is light and fluffy. By hand, stir in 1 egg, 1 tablespoon of the flour, and ½ teaspoon of the vanilla. Mix to blend and set aside.

With the electric mixer on medium speed, beat the remaining 2 eggs in a medium bowl until they are light and fluffy. Gradually add the remaining ¾ cup of sugar, and beat until the mixture is thickened, about 1 minute. Remove and fold in the remaining ½ cup of flour, the baking powder, and salt. Stir in the cooled chocolate mixture, the walnuts, and the remaining 1 teaspoon of vanilla. Pour this batter into the prepared pan.

Drizzle the reserved cream cheese mixture over the chocolate batter in the pan and use a spatula to swirl it into the chocolate batter to create a marbled effect. Bake the brownies until a tester comes out clean, about 30 minutes. Remove them from the oven and cool them to room temperature.

To make the icing: Put the chocolate, cream, and coffee in a heavy, medium saucepan over very low heat. Stir constantly until the mixture is smooth and creamy. Cool 15 minutes. Use a spatula to spread the icing over the top of the brownies. Refrigerate them until the icing is firm. Slice the brownies into 16 squares and store them in a covered container in the refrigerator. (The brownies can be prepared 2 days ahead. Bring them to room temperature 30 minutes before serving.)

MAKES 16 BROWNIES

Mocha Cheesecake Bars

For this recipe, a chocolate- and coffee-scented cheesecake batter is baked in a square baking pan that has been coated with a hazelnut and chocolate cookie crumb crust. After baking, the cheesecake is cut into attractive bars that are garnished with a dollop of whipped cream and sprinkled with cookie crumbs.

CRUST

¾ cup finely ground chocolate wafer cookies, plus 2 to 3 teaspoons for garnish

¾ cup ground toasted hazelnuts (toasted for 8 minutes in a 350°F oven, skins rubbed off, and nuts coarsely ground)

3 tablespoons unsalted butter, melted, plus extra for greasing baking dish

MOCHA CHEESECAKE

1½ teaspoons powdered instant espresso (see Note)

¼ cup hot water

6 ounces cream cheese, at room temperature

¾ cup sugar

2½ ounces semisweet chocolate, melted, plus a 2-ounce piece for garnish (optional)

1 cup sour cream

3 large eggs

½ cup heavy or whipping cream, whipped to firm peaks (optional)

Arrange an oven rack at center position and preheat the oven to 350 degrees F. Butter an 8-inch square baking dish.

To make the crust: In a medium bowl, toss together the ¾ cup of ground wafers, hazelnuts, and butter until thoroughly moistened. Transfer the mixture to the prepared baking dish and press it evenly into the bottom of the pan.

To make the Mocha Cheesecake layer: Put the coffee in a small heat-proof bowl and add the water. Stir to combine and set aside.

With an electric mixer on medium speed, beat the cream cheese in a medium bowl a few seconds, then add the sugar in a thin stream, beating until the mixture is smooth and creamy, 3 to 4 minutes. On low speed, add the coffee, and mix until it is just incorporated. Add the 2½ ounces of chocolate and mix until it is smooth. Then add the sour cream and beat until the mixture is creamy. Finally add the eggs and beat just until they are incorporated.

Pour the mixture into the prepared dish and bake 35 minutes. Turn off the oven and leave the dish in the oven with the door shut for 30 minutes. Remove the dish from the oven and let it cool to room temperature. Cover and refrigerate until it is chilled and set, 4 hours or overnight.

To serve, use a sharp knife and cut the baked cheesecake in half. Then, cut each half into 4 equal bars. Using a metal spatula, carefully remove the bars from the baking pan. (If not using immediately, transfer the bars to a platter, cover tightly with plastic wrap, and refrigerate for up to 1 day.) Garnish each bar with a dollop of whipped cream and a sprinkle of cookie crumbs. If desired, use a sharp knife or a vegetable peeler to shave some chocolate curls from a piece of chocolate and sprinkle the curls over the bars.

MAKES 8 BARS

Note:
Medaglia d'Oro makes an instant espresso coffee. If you can't find instant espresso, try to use a strong instant coffee such as Café Bustelo.

Chocolate-Pecan Phyllo Cups with Coffee Whipped Cream

"Little bites of heaven" is how I would describe these easy and quick confections. A quickly assembled mixture of melted butter, instant coffee, brown sugar, pecans, and chocolate chips is mounded in mini phyllo cups, then baked until the filling melts and melds together. These scrumptious little pastries, which can be served warm from the oven or at room temperature, are even better when garnished with swirls of coffee-scented whipped cream.

24 frozen mini phyllo cups, thawed in the refrigerator

5½ tablespoons (⅔ stick) unsalted butter

½ cup packed dark brown sugar

2 teaspoons powdered instant coffee

2 cups chopped pecans

6 ounces semisweet chocolate chips

GARNISH

1 teaspoon powdered instant coffee

1 teaspoon vanilla extract

¾ cup heavy or whipping cream

4 teaspoons confectioners' sugar

Place an oven rack at center position and preheat the oven to 350 degrees F. Arrange the phyllo cups on an ungreased baking sheet.

In a large, heavy skillet set over medium-high heat, melt the butter and stir in the brown sugar and coffee. Stir constantly, until the sugar and coffee have both dissolved. Add the pecans and stir just to coat them in the sugar mixture. Remove the skillet from the heat and stir in the chocolate. Mix well. The chocolate will start to melt slightly.

Spoon the chocolate and pecan mixture into each of the phyllo cups, filling them almost to the top. Bake until the phyllo is golden and the filling has melded together, about 7 minutes. Remove them from the oven and cool 10 minutes. (The phyllo cups can be prepared 1 day ahead; store them in an airtight container at cool room temperature.)

To make the garnish: Combine the coffee and vanilla in a small bowl, and stir until the coffee has dissolved. Add the cream. With an electric mixer (a small, hand-held one works particularly well for this recipe), whip the cream until soft peaks form. Add the confectioners' sugar and continue beating until firm, but not stiff. (The whipped cream can be prepared 6 hours ahead; cover and refrigerate.)

Serve the phyllo cups warm or at room temperature. Top each cup with a dollop of the whipped cream. You will probably have some whipped cream left over; it is great used as a garnish for hot or iced coffee.

MAKES 24 PHYLLO CUPS

Ginger Twists

Only three ingredients are needed to make these thin, flaky pastry sticks. A sheet of purchased puff pastry is rolled into a rectangle, sprinkled with chopped crystallized ginger, and then folded in half. This process is repeated several times, then long thin strips are cut from the pastry sheet, twisted, and baked. The golden baked twists, which are sprinkled with sugar, are perfect for dipping in cups of hot coffee.

¼ cup crystallized ginger pieces

1 frozen puff pastry sheet (half of a 17¼-ounce package), defrosted in the refrigerator (see Note)

Flour for dusting work surface

Granulated sugar for sprinkling

Place the ginger pieces in the bowl of a food processor and pulse until the ginger is finely chopped, for several seconds. Remove and set aside.

Roll the pastry on a lightly floured work surface into a 16-by-10-inch rectangle. (The pastry will be thin.) With a long side of the pastry sheet in front of you, sprinkle half of the chopped ginger evenly over the right half of the pastry; fold the other pastry half over the ginger, forming an 8-by-10-inch rectangle. Using your fingers, press down firmly on the top pastry sheet so that it adheres to the one below. Repeat, rolling the dough into a 16-by-10-inch rectangle, sprinkling the right half with the remaining ginger, and folding and pressing again. Roll out the pastry one final time to a 16-by-10-inch rectangle and transfer it to a baking sheet. Refrigerate it for 30 minutes.

Position 1 oven rack in the top third and 1 in the bottom third of the oven and preheat it to 425 degrees F.

Line 2 baking sheets with parchment paper. Trim and discard any uneven edges from the pastry dough. Then cut (from the short sides) ½-inch-wide strips from the dough. You should get 20 to 24 strips.

Holding each end, twist each strip a few times and place it on a prepared baking sheet, spacing the strips about 1 inch apart. Dab the ends of the strips with a drop or two of water and then press and smear the ends so that they adhere to the parchment. (Pressing and smearing the ends will help keep the pastries twisted during baking.)

Bake the twists 5 minutes, then reverse the baking sheets top to bottom. Continue to bake until the twists are golden brown, about 5 minutes more. Watch carefully so they do not burn.

(continued)

Remove the baking sheets from the oven, and sprinkle the twists lightly with a little sugar. Cool the twists on the baking sheets 10 minutes, then serve or finish cooling them on a rack. (The twists can be made 2 days ahead; store them in an airtight container at room temperature.)

To serve, arrange the twists in a napkin-lined basket or in wide-rimmed wine goblets or other decorative glasses.

MAKES 20 TO 24 TWISTS

Note:
Pepperidge Farm makes good puff pastry dough, which is available in most groceries in the freezer section.

Irish Coffee–Chocolate Tart

While working on this tart's chocolate filling, flavored with Irish whiskey and coffee, I had trouble getting the cooked egg yolks and melted chocolate to combine properly. I called Shirley Corriher, food chemist extraordinaire and friend. She walked me through each step to achieve a perfectly smooth and marbled chocolate mixture, which I then poured into a golden pastry shell. This tart is rich and satisfying, so you might want to serve small slices.

CRUST

1½ cups all-purpose flour, plus extra for rolling

2 tablespoons confectioners' sugar

Pinch of salt

5 tablespoons (⅔ stick) unsalted butter, chilled and cut into small pieces

2½ tablespoons solid vegetable shortening, chilled and cut into small pieces

About 4 tablespoons ice water

FILLING

⅔ cup granulated sugar

1⅓ cups heavy or whipping cream, divided

4 large egg yolks

4 ounces semisweet chocolate, finely chopped, plus 1 ounce for garnish (optional)

2 ounces unsweetened chocolate, finely chopped

1 tablespoon powdered instant coffee

5 tablespoons Irish whiskey, divided

To make the crust: Put the flour, confectioners' sugar, and salt in a food processor, and add the butter and shortening. Process, pulsing several times, until the mixture resembles coarse meal. With the machine running, slowly add the water just until moist clumps form. Remove the dough and gather it into a ball; flatten it into a disk. Wrap the dough in plastic wrap and refrigerate it 30 minutes before using. (The dough can be made 1 day ahead; soften it slightly at room temperature before using.)

Roll the dough out on a lightly floured work surface into a 12-inch round. Transfer it to a 9-inch tart pan with a removable bottom. Trim any overhanging dough to 1 inch. Fold the overhanging dough in and press it to itself to form double-thick sides. Prick the bottom of the crust all over with the tines of a fork. Cover and freeze it 30 minutes.

(continued)

Arrange an oven rack at center position and preheat the oven to 400 degrees F.

Bake the crust until it is golden brown, piercing the bottom with a fork if it bubbles, 30 to 35 minutes. Transfer the crust to a cooling rack and cool it to room temperature.

To make the filling: Whisk the granulated sugar, ⅓ cup of the cream, and the egg yolks together in a medium heat-proof bowl set over (but not touching) a pot of simmering water. Whisk constantly until the sugar has dissolved and small bubbles form around the edge of the bowl, 3 to 4 minutes. Remove it from the heat and stir in the 4 ounces of semisweet chocolate, the unsweetened chocolate, coffee, and 4 tablespoons of the whiskey. Whisk until the mixture is smooth and shiny. Cool it to room temperature.

With an electric mixer on medium-high speed, whip the remaining 1 cup of cream in a medium bowl until soft peaks form. Add the remaining 1 tablespoon of whiskey and beat until the cream is firm. Fold half of the whipped cream into the chocolate mixture, taking care not to blend it completely so that you create a marbled effect. Spread the filling evenly in the cooled tart shell and swirl it with a knife to marble it some more. Refrigerate until the filling is firm, at least 2 hours or up to 6 hours. Cover and refrigerate the remaining whipped cream separately.

Serve each slice with a dollop of the reserved whipped cream and, if desired, with a shaving of chocolate.

MAKES 8 TO 10 SERVINGS

Cranberry Upside-Down Cake

For this dessert, cranberries that have been tossed in an orange-flavored sugar syrup are arranged in a single layer in a cake pan, then a batter scented with orange and cardamom is poured over them. After baking, the cake is removed from the pan and inverted so that the cooked berries are on top and form a beautiful glistening crown. Served warm or at room temperature, this dessert is delicious offered with scoops of vanilla ice cream and cups of hot coffee.

Butter for greasing cake pan

CRANBERRIES

½ cup granulated sugar

2 tablespoons freshly squeezed
  orange juice

1 tablespoon unsalted butter

1½ cups fresh cranberries or frozen,
  thawed, and patted dry

½ teaspoon grated orange zest

CAKE

8 tablespoons (1 stick) unsalted
  butter, at room temperature

¾ cup granulated sugar

1 cup all-purpose flour

2 large eggs, lightly beaten

2 teaspoons grated orange zest

1½ teaspoons baking powder

¾ teaspoon ground cardamom

Pinch of salt

Confectioners' sugar for serving

Arrange an oven rack at center position and preheat the oven to 350 degrees F. Generously butter an 8-inch straight-sided cake pan and set it aside.

To make the cranberry layer: Combine the ½ cup granulated sugar and orange juice in a medium, heavy saucepan over medium heat. Cook and stir until the sugar dissolves, 1 minute or less. Add the butter and cook until it melts, a few seconds more. Remove the pan from the heat and add the cranberries and ½ teaspoon zest. Stir to coat them well. Spoon the berries in a single layer into the prepared pan.

To make the cake layer: With an electric mixer on medium speed, cream the butter and ¾ cup granulated sugar in a medium bowl until they are smooth and creamy, 3 to 4 minutes. Reduce the speed to low, and add the flour, eggs, 2 teaspoons zest, baking powder, cardamom, and salt. Beat just until everything is combined. Pour the batter over the cranberries in the

(continued)

pan, using a spatula to smooth the top evenly. Bake until a tester inserted into the center comes out clean, 40 to 50 minutes. Remove the pan from the oven and cool it 10 minutes.

To unmold, run a small knife around the inside edge of the cake pan. Cover the pan with a flat plate and invert. The cake can be served warm or at room temperature, but is best served the day it is made. If not serving it immediately, cool and leave it at room temperature, covered with a cake dome or tented loosely with aluminum foil.

To serve, dust the cake with confectioners' sugar and slice it into portions.

MAKES 6 TO 8 SERVINGS

Walnut-Orange Cake with Orange–Cream Cheese Frosting

This single-layer cake is moist, light, tender, and permeated with the taste of walnuts and orange. Covered with an Orange–Cream cheese frosting, this confection makes a perfect partner to serve with a cup of steaming hot New Orleans Café Brûlot (page 27) or with Holiday Spiced Coffee with Brandied Whipped Cream (page 22).

CAKE

12 tablespoons (1½ sticks) unsalted butter, at room temperature, plus extra for greasing baking pan

1¼ cups granulated sugar

3 large egg yolks

2 teaspoons vanilla extract

2 cups (8 ounces) walnuts, finely ground to a coarse powder

1½ tablespoons grated orange zest

½ cup plus 2 tablespoons all-purpose flour, plus extra for dusting baking pan

6 large egg whites

Pinch of salt

FROSTING

4 ounces (½ cup) cream cheese, at room temperature

3 tablespoons unsalted butter, at room temperature

1½ cups confectioners' sugar

1½ teaspoons freshly squeezed orange juice

1½ teaspoons grated orange zest

8 walnut halves

Arrange an oven rack at center position and preheat the oven to 350 degrees F. Butter and flour an 8- or 8½-inch springform pan.

To make the cake: With an electric mixer on high speed, beat the butter and granulated sugar together in a large bowl until they are light and fluffy, about 5 minutes. Add the egg yolks and vanilla and beat another 3 minutes. Reduce the speed to low, and add the ground walnuts and 1½ tablespoons zest. When the walnuts and zest are blended into the mixture, add the flour and beat just until it is blended in. Set aside.

With the electric mixer on high speed and with clean beaters, beat the egg whites with a pinch of salt in a large bowl until they are just firm and soft peaks form, about 2 minutes. Stir 1 cup of the egg whites into the yolk mixture to lighten it. Then fold in the remaining egg whites, in 3 equal additions.

(continued)

Pour the batter into the prepared pan and bake until a cake tester comes out dry and the top of the cake springs back when lightly touched, about 50 minutes. Remove it from the oven and cool it to room temperature. Then run a knife around the inside edge of the pan and remove the sides of the pan.

To make the frosting: With the electric mixer on medium-high speed, cream together the cream cheese and butter in a medium bowl until they are well blended, about 1 minute. Reduce the speed to medium, add the confectioners' sugar gradually, and continue beating until the mixture is smooth, about 2 minutes. Beat in the orange juice and zest.

With a spatula, ice the top and sides of the cake, and arrange the walnut halves equidistant around the top edge of the cake. (The cake can be prepared 1 day ahead. Cover it with a cake dome or tent it loosely with aluminum foil and refrigerate. Bring it to room temperature 30 minutes before serving.)

MAKES 8 SERVINGS

Light as Air Cake with Coffee–Toffee Icing

Tall and stately, this big, incredibly light sponge cake is frosted with a custard icing flavored with coffee and toffee bits. The cake takes a little extra time to prepare, but it serves a crowd and is perfect for a special occasion when you want to invite people to come simply for dessert and coffee. Since this cake can be prepared a day ahead, there's no last-minute worry.

CAKE

1½ teaspoons powdered instant coffee

3 tablespoons hot water

7 large eggs, separated, at room temperature

1 cup sugar, divided

1 teaspoon vanilla extract

¾ teaspoon cream of tartar

1 cup cake flour

¼ teaspoon salt

COFFEE–TOFFEE ICING

½ cup chilled brewed coffee (see Note, page 29)

2 teaspoons powdered instant coffee

1 envelope (2 generous teaspoons) unflavored gelatin

2½ cups heavy or whipping cream, divided

5 large egg yolks

⅔ cup sugar

1½ cups toffee bits (see Note)

8 to 10 chocolate-coated coffee beans (optional)

Arrange an oven rack at center position and preheat the oven to 325 degrees F. Line the bottom of a 9-inch springform pan with parchment paper cut to fit. Do not grease the paper or pan.

To make the cake: Dissolve the coffee in the water and set it aside. With an electric mixer on medium-high speed, beat the 7 egg yolks in a large bowl, gradually adding ⅔ cup of the sugar in a thin stream. Continue to beat until the mixture is thick and pale yellow, 2 to 3 minutes. Reduce the speed and add the coffee and vanilla.

With the electric mixer on medium-high speed and with clean beaters, beat the 7 egg whites in a large bowl until they are frothy. Add the cream of tartar, and when the egg whites start to mound, gradually add the remaining ⅓ cup of sugar. Continue beating until the whites are just stiff and hold peaks, 2 to 3 minutes or longer.

(continued)

Sift the flour and salt into the bowl with the egg yolk mixture, then fold them in until no traces of flour remain. Fold in the egg whites in 2 equal additions. Pour the batter into the prepared pan and smooth it with a spatula.

Bake until the cake is golden and springs back when touched, 40 to 45 minutes. As it bakes, the cake will rise above the rim of the pan. Have ready 4 glasses that will be used as a stand for the cake to rest on when it is inverted to cool.

Remove the pan from the oven, and invert it so that the pan rests upside down on the 4 glasses. Cool the cake in the pan completely, about 1½ hours.

Run a knife around the inside edge of the pan, and remove the pan sides. Invert the cake (bottom side up) onto a platter. Remove the parchment. With a serrated knife, cut the cake into 2 equal layers.

To make the icing: Put the brewed coffee in a small bowl and stir in the instant coffee until it is dissolved. Sprinkle the gelatin over the mixture.

Heat 1½ cups of the cream in a small heat-proof bowl set over (but not touching) a pot of simmering water, until it is just warm to the touch. Remove it from the heat.

Whisk the egg yolks in a medium bowl until they are blended, 1 minute or more. Gradually whisk in the sugar, then the warm cream. Return the mixture to the heat-proof bowl set over simmering water and whisk constantly until the mixture thickens and coats the back of a spoon, about 10 minutes. Remove and stir in the coffee and gelatin mixture. Refrigerate until it is cool, but not set, about 30 minutes.

With the electric mixer on medium-high speed, beat the remaining 1 cup of cream until it is just firm, then fold it into the chilled custard. Spread the bottom layer of the cake with 1½ cups of the icing, then sprinkle 1 cup of the toffee bits over it. Place the remaining cake layer on top and spread the rest of the icing over the top and sides. Make a border on the top of the cake with the remaining ½ cup of toffee bits. Garnish the top of the cake with coffee beans arranged on top of the toffee border, if desired. Transfer the cake to a serving platter and refrigerate it, tented loosely with aluminum foil or with a cake dome, for 3 hours or up to 1 day.

MAKES 12 TO 14 SERVINGS

Note:
Toffee bits can usually be found in the baking section of the grocery. Heath Bits 'O Brickle is a well-known brand that is widely available. Don't use chocolate-coated toffee bits.

CREAMY

COFFEE CONFECTIONS

COFFEE AND CREAM, JUST LIKE COFFEE AND SUGAR, HAVE

had a love affair for a long time. The silken smoothness of cream enhances coffee immeasurably and is included in all the desserts in this chapter. Puddings and custards infused with coffee, luscious Coffee Caramels, and a cooling coffee ice crowned with whipped cream—these are just some of the temptations you'll discover in this chapter.

Among the legions of crèmes brûlées, a coffee-scented version is a delectable and new variation. In the pudding category, you can also try the Chocolate–Espresso Pots de Crème topped with White Chocolate Whipped Cream.

Nothing compares to homemade ice cream, and the Best Ever Coffee Ice Cream will

not disappoint. You can devour it unadorned or gild the lily by drizzling it with either Warm Chocolate Sauce or Coffee–Caramel Sauce. You can also use it to make the delightful Coffee Ice Cream Sandwiches or as a filling for those wonderful little cream puffs known as profiteroles.

Some old favorites get new twists in this section. You'll find a tiramisu, Italy's coffee-scented trifle, made in individual ramekins rather than in the traditional single large pan. And truffles, those rich confections of chocolate and cream, are packed here with a triple jolt of coffee flavor.

Chocolate–Espresso Pots de Crème with White Chocolate Whipped Cream

Chocolate and coffee make perfect partners in these delectable, dark chocolate pots de crème flavored with a hint of espresso. A topping of white chocolate whipped cream takes these silky smooth puddings to new heights. Serve them with cups of piping hot espresso.

2 cups heavy or whipping cream

4 ounces semisweet chocolate, coarsely chopped

1 teaspoon powdered instant espresso (see Note, page 55)

6 large egg yolks

3 tablespoons sugar

⅛ teaspoon salt

WHITE CHOCOLATE WHIPPED CREAM

1½ ounces white chocolate, coarsely chopped

½ cup plus 2 tablespoons heavy or whipping cream, divided

1 ounce semisweet chocolate, at room temperature (optional)

Arrange an oven rack at center position and preheat the oven to 325 degrees F. Put six ½-cup ramekins, soufflés, or custard cups in a large, shallow baking pan.

Put the cream, the 4 ounces of semisweet chocolate, and espresso in a heavy, medium saucepan over low heat and whisk constantly, until the chocolate and coffee are dissolved and small bubbles form around the edge of the pan. Remove the pan from the heat and cool 5 minutes.

With an electric mixer on medium speed, beat the egg yolks in a medium bowl until they are well combined. Gradually add the sugar and salt and continue to beat until the mixture is slightly thickened and light in color, about 1 minute. Do not overbeat the mixture. On low speed, slowly pour in the reserved cream and chocolate mixture. Mix just to incorporate them.

Transfer the mixture to a medium heat-proof bowl set over (but not touching) a pot of simmering water. Stir constantly for 2 minutes. Pour the mixture through a fine mesh sieve into the prepared ramekins. Pour enough hot water into the large baking pan to come halfway up the sides of the ramekins. Carefully transfer the pan to the oven. Bake until the custards are just set, about 25 minutes. The centers of the custards should still be a little quivery.

(continued)

Meanwhile, make the White Chocolate Whipped Cream: Put the white chocolate and 2 tablespoons of the cream in the top of a small heat-proof bowl set over (but not touching) a pot of simmering water. Whisk constantly until the chocolate is smooth and creamy. Remove the bowl and set it aside to cool 10 minutes.

With the electric mixer on medium speed, beat the remaining ½ cup of cream in a medium bowl until soft peaks form. Reduce the speed and pour in the cooled white chocolate mixture. Continue to beat until stiff peaks form. Cover and refrigerate. (The White Chocolate Whipped Cream can be prepared 1 day ahead.) Makes about 1¼ cups.

When the custards are set, remove the ramekins to a rack, and cool them to room temperature. Cover and refrigerate them until chilled. (The pots de crème can be made 1 day ahead.)

Serve each pot de crème with a dollop of White Chocolate Whipped Cream and, if desired, garnish each serving with a shaving of chocolate.

MAKES 6 SERVINGS

Best Ever Coffee Ice Cream

This ice cream, which falls in the decadent category, is rich, velvety smooth, and completely satisfying. It can stand alone, scooped into a bowl or a wineglass, or you can drizzle Warm Chocolate Sauce or Coffee–Caramel Sauce over it for added indulgence.

⅔ cup sugar

4 large egg yolks

Pinch of salt

1⅓ cups heavy or whipping cream

1 cup whole milk

3 tablespoons powdered instant coffee

½ teaspoon vanilla extract

Warm Chocolate Sauce (page 85)
  or Coffee–Caramel Sauce (page 88)
  (optional)

Whisk together the sugar, egg yolks, and salt in a medium heat-proof bowl until they are blended. Set aside.

Combine the cream and milk in a medium, heavy saucepan set over medium-high heat. Heat until small bubbles form around the edge of the pan. Add the coffee and whisk until it is completely dissolved. Remove the pan from the heat. Gradually whisk the warm cream mixture into the egg yolks. Return the mixture to the saucepan, set it over medium-low heat, and stir constantly until the mixture coats the back of a spoon, about 5 minutes. Stir in the vanilla. Pour the custard mixture back into the bowl and put it in a larger bowl filled with ice. Refrigerate the custard until it is cold, stirring occasionally, about 1 hour.

Place the chilled mixture in an ice cream machine and process according to the manufacturer's directions. Pack the ice cream into a container and freeze until ready to serve. If the ice cream is frozen solid, transfer it to the refrigerator for 15 minutes to soften slightly before serving.

Serve scoops of the ice cream in bowls or wineglasses and drizzle them, if desired, with some Warm Chocolate Sauce or Coffee–Caramel Sauce.

MAKES ABOUT 1½ PINTS

Corby Kummer's Granita di Caffè

Coffee aficionado Corby Kummer shared his delectable recipe for this celebrated Italian dessert with me. As he writes in his book *The Joy of Coffee,* "No dessert in all Italy is better than the shaved coffee ice at the Tazza d'Oro, the best espresso bar in Rome." This is his version of that establishment's popular confection. You freeze sweetened coffee in a shallow pan, and as the mixture starts to set, you make frequent trips to the freezer to stir and scrape the icy mixture with a fork. The granita is served in chilled glasses and topped with whipped cream. Dessert and coffee all in one!

3¼ cups water, divided

½ cup sugar

6 tablespoons ground coffee, such as Colombian or a house blend

1 teaspoon vanilla extract

½ cup heavy or whipping cream, lightly whipped

In a small saucepan, combine 1 cup of the water and the sugar over medium heat, and stir until the sugar dissolves. Pour the sugar syrup into a small heat-proof bowl and refrigerate until it is cold.

Brew the coffee, preferably in an automatic drip coffeemaker, using the remaining 2¼ cups of water. Combine the cooled sugar syrup and coffee in a medium bowl and stir in the vanilla. Pour the mixture into a freezer-safe pan, such as a 9-by-13-inch metal pan.

Freeze, stirring the mixture with a rubber spatula after 30 minutes. Then stir every 30 minutes with the tines of a fork until the mixture is completely frozen and of a grainy consistency, 3 to 4 hours. (Granita is best served the day it is made, but can be made 1 day ahead and kept covered in the freezer. Stir it with a fork to loosen before serving.)

To serve, spoon a cup of granita into each of 6 chilled martini glasses, wineglasses, or other decorative glasses and top with a dollop of whipped cream.

MAKES 6 SERVINGS

Crèmes Brûlées au Café

Crèmes brûlées would definitely earn a spot on America's top-ten hit parade of desserts. In this version, coffee adds a new dimension of flavor and a depth of color to these creamy baked custards with their crunchy, caramelized sugar topping.

2 cups heavy or whipping cream

½ cup granulated sugar

1 tablespoon powdered instant coffee

5 large eggs yolks

3 tablespoons packed light brown sugar

Arrange an oven rack at center position and preheat the oven to 325 degrees F. Place six ¾-cup ramekins in a large, shallow baking pan.

Mix the cream, granulated sugar, and coffee in a heavy, medium saucepan. Stir them over medium heat until the sugar dissolves and the mixture comes to a simmer. Strain it through a fine-mesh sieve into a large measuring cup with a spout.

Whisk the egg yolks in a medium heat-proof bowl until they are well blended. Gradually whisk in the hot cream mixture just to blend. Return the custard to the measuring cup; divide it evenly among the ramekins. Pour enough hot water into the pan to come halfway up the sides of the ramekins. Carefully transfer the pan to the oven.

Bake the custards until they are almost set in the center when the pan is gently shaken, 30 to 35 minutes. Remove the ramekins from the pan and let them cool for 30 minutes before covering them with plastic wrap. Refrigerate them at least 3 hours or up to 2 days.

To serve the brûlées, sprinkle 1½ teaspoons brown sugar evenly over each custard. Preheat the broiler and arrange the ramekins on a baking sheet. Broil them 1 minute or less, just until the sugar melts. (If you have a kitchen blowtorch, use it according to the manufacturer's directions to melt the sugar on top of the ramekins.)

MAKES 6 SERVINGS

Emily's Frozen Coffee Cup Soufflés

My good friend and longtime assistant, Emily Bell from Columbus, Ohio, created these scrumptious frozen coffee soufflés, which she serves in coffee cups. She describes them as "having your coffee and eating it too!"

1½ cups heavy or whipping cream, divided

1½ tablespoons powdered instant espresso (see Note, page 55)

¼ teaspoon ground cinnamon

3 large egg yolks

6 tablespoons sugar

2 ounces semisweet chocolate coarsely grated, divided

4 standard-size freezer-proof coffee cups

Put ½ cup of the cream, the espresso, and cinnamon in a small saucepan. Stir to mix them well. Then set the pan over very low heat and stir or whisk constantly until the espresso and cinnamon are completely dissolved in the cream. Remove the pan from the heat and set it aside to cool to room temperature.

In a medium heat-proof bowl, combine the egg yolks and sugar and whisk until they are blended. Stir in the cooled cream mixture. Set the bowl over (but not touching) a pot of simmering water. Whisk constantly until the mixture thickens slightly and coats the back of a spoon, about 5 minutes. Remove and refrigerate the mixture until it is chilled, about 40 minutes.

When the custard is chilled, remove it from the refrigerator. With an electric mixer on high speed, beat the remaining 1 cup of cream in a large bowl just until firm peaks form. Stir 2 tablespoons of the whipped cream into the custard, then fold in the remaining cream in 2 additions. Fold half of the grated chocolate into the custard. Then spoon the mixture into the 4 coffee cups.

Cover each cup with plastic wrap and freeze until the soufflés are set, 3 hours or longer. (The frozen soufflés can be prepared 5 days ahead; store them covered with plastic wrap in the freezer.) Thirty minutes before you plan to serve them, transfer the soufflés to the refrigerator to soften slightly, then sprinkle each with some of the remaining grated chocolate.

MAKES 4 SERVINGS

Individual Tiramisus

Tiramisu (which translates as "pull me up") is one of Italy's most celebrated desserts. Made by layering coffee-soaked ladyfingers or sponge cake with sweetened mascarpone, this confection is usually assembled in a large pan. In the following version, individual portions are prepared in ½-cup ramekins, a practical alternative to the original. Serve these tiramisus with cups of hot espresso.

1 cup brewed espresso, cooled

¼ cup Kahlúa or other coffee liqueur

3 large egg yolks (see Note, page 33)

5 tablespoons sugar, divided

1½ cups mascarpone cheese

2 teaspoons vanilla extract

2 large egg whites

12 soft ladyfingers
 (about 1 by 3½ inches)

1 tablespoon shaved bittersweet or
 semisweet chocolate

Pour the espresso into a small shallow bowl and the Kahlúa into a separate small bowl. Have ready six ½-cup ramekins.

With an electric mixer on medium-high speed, beat the egg yolks with 4 tablespoons of the sugar in a large bowl, until the mixture is thick and pale yellow, 4 to 5 minutes. Reduce the speed to low and beat in the mascarpone and vanilla until they are well combined.

With the electric mixer on high speed and clean beaters, beat the egg whites with the remaining 1 tablespoon of sugar in a medium bowl until soft peaks form, about 1 minute. Lightly fold the egg whites into the mascarpone mixture.

Split the ladyfingers lengthwise, and cut them to fit the ramekins. Dip the sliced ladyfingers, 1 at a time, into the espresso. Line the bottom of the ramekins with enough ladyfingers to make a single layer. Drizzle1 teaspoon of the Kahlúa over the ladyfingers in each ramekin, then cover them with ¼ cup of the mascarpone mixture. Repeat, making another ladyfinger and mascarpone layer in each ramekin. Sprinkle ½ teaspoon of the shaved chocolate on top of each tiramisu.

Cover the ramekins with plastic wrap and refrigerate them at least 2 hours or up to 4 hours. Serve cold.

MAKES 6 SERVINGS

Profiteroles with Coffee Ice Cream and Warm Chocolate Sauce

A classic French dessert, profiteroles are small cream puffs prepared with *pâte à choux* dough. They are always crowd pleasers and not difficult to prepare. The thick dough is made by adding butter, flour, and eggs to hot water. Then the dough is transferred to a pastry bag and small mounds of it are piped onto a baking sheet. Baked until golden and puffed, the pastries are split and often filled with ice cream. For this version, I used coffee ice cream and drizzled the profiteroles with Warm Chocolate Sauce. Coffee–Caramel Sauce (page 88) would also be delicious served with these little treats.

1 cup plus ½ teaspoon water, divided

8 tablespoons (1 stick) unsalted butter, cut into small pieces

1 cup all-purpose flour, sifted

¼ teaspoon salt

5 large eggs, divided

WARM CHOCOLATE SAUCE
1 cup heavy or whipping cream

8 ounces semisweet chocolate, chopped

4 cups (1 quart) coffee ice cream, either homemade (page 77) or good-quality purchased

Confectioners' sugar for garnish

Equipment needed: a pastry bag fitted with a ½-inch plain tip

Arrange an oven rack at center position and preheat the oven to 425 degrees F. Have ready a large, ungreased baking sheet.

Put 1 cup of the water and the butter in a medium saucepan set over high heat. Bring them to a boil and heat until the butter has melted. Remove the pan from the heat, and add the flour and salt all at once. Stir constantly with a wooden spoon until they are blended in, several seconds. Return the pan to medium-high heat, and continue to stir until the mixture is smooth and leaves the sides of the pan, forming a mass of dough, about 1 minute. Remove the pan from the heat and let it rest 5 minutes.

Beat 4 of the eggs lightly in a small bowl. Transfer the dough (which will still be warm) to a food processor and process it for 5 to 10 seconds.

(continued)

With the machine going, add the eggs all at once through the feed tube, and process until the dough is smooth and well blended, 20 to 30 seconds.

Spoon the dough into a pastry bag fitted with a ½-inch plain tip. On the baking sheet, pipe 16 mounds that are 1½ to 2 inches wide and about 1½ inches tall at the highest point, spacing them 1 inch apart. Mix the remaining egg and ½ teaspoon of water in a small bowl. Brush the mounds lightly with this mixture, then flatten the top of each mound lightly with the brush.

Bake until the puffs have doubled in size and are lightly browned, 20 minutes. Reduce the heat to 375 degrees F and bake until the puffs are golden brown and crusty to the touch, 8 to 10 minutes more.

Meanwhile, make the chocolate sauce: Put the cream in a medium, heavy saucepan over medium-high heat. Bring it to a boil. Remove it from the heat and add the chocolate. Whisk until the mixture is smooth and shiny. (The chocolate sauce can be prepared 5 days ahead. Cool, cover, and refrigerate. Reheat, stirring, over medium-low heat.) Makes 1 cup.

Remove the puffs from the oven and turn off the oven. With a sharp knife, make a 1-inch slit in the side of each puff. Return the puffs to the hot, turned-off oven and leave the door ajar for 5 minutes. Remove the puffs from the oven and cut the tops off. With a teaspoon, scrape out and discard any uncooked dough inside the puffs. (The puffs can be prepared 1 day ahead; store them in an airtight container at room temperature.)

To serve, fill each puff with a large scoop of coffee ice cream, then drizzle it with a little Warm Chocolate Sauce and replace the top. Place 2 puffs on each of 8 dessert plates and drizzle them with some more Warm Chocolate Sauce and dust them with confectioners' sugar.

MAKES 8 SERVINGS

Coffee Ice Cream Sandwiches

A scoop of coffee ice cream pressed between two butter-rich Cappuccino Icebox Cookies results in a delectable ice cream sandwich. For an extra flourish, I drizzle the cookies with a little melted chocolate. When they are put in a tightly sealed plastic bag, the sandwiches can be stored for up to 2 weeks in the freezer.

2 cups (1 pint) coffee ice cream, either homemade (page 77) or purchased

12 Cappuccino Icebox Cookies (page 45), preferably baked without almonds

¼ cup heavy or whipping cream

2 ounces semisweet chocolate, chopped

Put the ice cream in the refrigerator 30 minutes before using it, to soften.

Place the cookies, flat sides down, on a baking sheet. Put the cream and chocolate in a small, heavy saucepan, and heat them over low heat, stirring constantly, until the chocolate melts. Drizzle the melted chocolate mixture in a zigzag pattern over each cookie, using a small spoon or a plastic pour bottle with a small tip. (If the chocolate starts to solidify, reheat it by setting the saucepan over low heat and stirring or, if using a plastic pour bottle, put it in a bowl of hot water for a few seconds.). Place the tray of chocolate-drizzled cookies in the freezer until the chocolate is completely firm and set.

To assemble a sandwich, place 1 cookie, decorated side down, on a flat surface. Put a small scoop (about 2 or more heaping tablespoons) of ice cream on it and top with another cookie, decorated side up. Press down gently to spread the ice cream evenly between the cookies. Repeat to make 5 more sandwiches. Place the sandwiches in a large self-sealing plastic bag and freeze them until ready to serve.

MAKES 6 SANDWICHES

Coffee–Caramel Sundaes

Alternating scoops of coffee and vanilla ice creams, topped with dark Coffee–Caramel Sauce, make these sundaes far from ordinary. The secret to their enticing flavor lies in the homemade sauce, which is prepared with a generous amount of cream and butter, brown and white sugars, and flavorings of vanilla and coffee. The sauce can be prepared three days ahead and used when needed.

COFFEE–CARAMEL SAUCE

1½ tablespoons powdered instant coffee

¼ cup hot water

2 teaspoons vanilla extract

1 cup heavy or whipping cream

¾ cup light corn syrup

½ cup packed light brown sugar

½ cup granulated sugar

6 tablespoons (¾ stick) unsalted butter, cut into small pieces

2 cups (1 pint) coffee ice cream, either homemade (page 77) or best-quality purchased

2 cups (1 pint) best-quality vanilla ice cream

Dissolve the coffee in a small bowl with the water. Then stir in the vanilla.

Put the cream, corn syrup, and sugars in a 3-quart heavy saucepan set over medium-low heat. Stir until the sugars dissolve and the mixture starts to boil. Continue to boil until the mixture is quite thick and coats the back of a spoon, about 10 minutes.

Remove the pan from the heat and stir in the coffee and vanilla mixture and the butter. Cool the sauce to room temperature, stirring occasionally to keep a skin from forming. (The sauce can be prepared 3 days ahead; when cool, cover and refrigerate it. Reheat it over low heat, stirring, until just barely warm.) Makes 2 cups.

To make the sundaes: Place a generous scoop of coffee ice cream in each of 4 sundae glasses or tall champagne flutes. Drizzle the ice cream with 2 tablespoons of the Coffee–Caramel Sauce. Add a generous scoop of vanilla ice cream and drizzle with 2 tablespoons more sauce. Repeat, adding 1 more coffee and 1 more vanilla scoop to each glass, and covering each with 2 tablespoons sauce. Serve immediately.

MAKES 4 SERVINGS

Walnut–Coffee Mousse Parfaits

To make these simple but attractive parfaits, a rich coffee custard is lightened with whipped cream, then mounded into wineglasses and layered with toasted walnuts. The mousses can be prepared a day ahead and are delicious accompanied by a Perfect Cup of Coffee (page 13).

1 tablespoon powdered instant coffee

2 tablespoons hot water

2 tablespoons Kahlúa or other coffee liqueur

4 large egg yolks

½ cup packed light brown sugar

1½ cups heavy or whipping cream

¾ cup walnuts, toasted for 5 minutes in a 350°F oven and chopped

Dissolve the coffee in the water in a small bowl. Stir in the Kahlúa. Set the mixture aside.

With an electric mixer on medium-high speed, beat the egg yolks in a large bowl until they are combined, several seconds. Gradually beat in the sugar, a little at a time, until it is well blended, 1 to 2 minutes. Reduce the speed to low, and beat in the coffee mixture.

Put the egg and coffee mixture in a medium heat-proof bowl set over (but not touching) a pot of simmering water, and whisk constantly until the mixture is quite thick and coats the back of a spoon, 4 to 5 minutes. Remove the bowl from the heat and refrigerate it, uncovered, until the mixture is cool, but not set, about 30 minutes.

With the electric mixer on high speed and with clean beaters, whip the cream in a large bowl until it is firm, but not stiff. Using a rubber spatula, gently fold the cream in 3 additions into the cooled egg and coffee mixture.

Ladle ¼ cup of the mousse into each of 4 medium-sized wineglasses. Sprinkle the mousse layer with 1 tablespoon of the walnuts. Repeat to make 2 more layers of mousse and walnuts in each glass. Cover the parfaits with plastic wrap and refrigerate them until firm, 2 hours or overnight. (Keep the mousses refrigerated until you are ready to serve since the whipped cream starts to soften quickly at room temperature.)

MAKES 4 SERVINGS

Java Jolt Truffles

There is a triple jolt of coffee flavoring in these luscious chocolate morsels. Instant coffee and coffee liqueur flavor a ganache of melted chocolate and cream. Then, crushed chocolate-coated coffee beans are stirred into the chilled and slightly set chocolate mixture. When you bite into one of these sublime candies, first you taste the creamy, smooth coffee-scented chocolate, then the crunch of the beans. It's likely that you won't be able to stop at just one!

8 ounces bittersweet
 (not unsweetened) chocolate,
 very finely chopped

½ cup plus 2 tablespoons heavy
 or whipping cream

1½ teaspoons powdered instant
 espresso (see Note, page 55)

2 tablespoons Kahlúa or other
 coffee liqueur

½ cup crushed dark chocolate–coated
 coffee beans (see Note)

¼ cup Dutch–process cocoa (see Note)

Put the chocolate into a large heat-proof bowl, and set it aside.

Put the cream and coffee in a heavy, medium saucepan set over medium-high heat. Whisk constantly, until the coffee dissolves and the cream comes to a boil. Immediately pour the cream over the chocolate and stir until the chocolate melts completely. If all of the chocolate doesn't melt, transfer the mixture back to the saucepan and heat it on low for a few seconds. Stir in the Kahlúa.

Spread the chocolate mixture in a pie plate or a shallow pan and refrigerate it until cool and slightly firm, about 30 minutes. Stir the crushed coffee beans into the chocolate mixture. Cover it with plastic wrap and return it to the refrigerator until the chocolate is cold and firm, 2 hours or overnight.

To shape the truffles, spread the cocoa on a dinner plate and have another dinner plate empty. Coat your hands with some cocoa and, with a teaspoon, scoop a heaping spoonful of the chocolate mixture into your hand. Shape it into a ball, then roll it in the cocoa powder, coating it on all sides. Place the truffle on the clean plate. Continue until all the chocolate has been shaped. Cover

(continued)

the truffles tightly with plastic wrap and refrigerate them for up to 1 week. Keep them refrigerated until serving.

Note:
Chocolate-coated coffee beans are available in some supermarkets and in specialty food stores. You will need a scant ½ cup to yield ½ cup crushed beans. To crush the beans, put them in a self-sealing plastic bag, and pound them with a meat pounder or heavy rolling pin.

Dutch–process cocoa is treated with an alkali, which helps to neutralize the cocoa's natural acidity. Droste is a readily available brand.

Coffee Caramels

In addition to the rich caramel taste of butter and sugar, these smooth, luscious candies have an accent of coffee. The addition of the latter turns these caramels a rich dark brown. Serve them with cups of espresso, latte, or cappuccino, and be prepared to eat more than one. These sweet little nibbles are addictive.

4 tablespoons (½ stick) unsalted butter, plus extra for greasing baking pan

2 teaspoons vanilla extract

2 tablespoons powdered instant coffee

¾ cup heavy or whipping cream

½ cup packed light brown sugar

½ cup granulated sugar

½ cup light corn syrup

Pinch of salt

Vegetable oil for cutting

Equipment needed:
  a candy thermometer

Line an 8-inch square baking pan with aluminum foil, with an overhang on 2 sides of about 2 inches. Generously butter the foil and sides of the pan. Set it aside.

Put the butter and vanilla in a small saucepan over medium heat. Stir until the butter has melted. Add the coffee and continue to stir until it is dissolved.

Remove the pan from the heat and set it aside. Do not worry if the coffee and the butter seem to separate.

Combine the cream, sugars, corn syrup, and salt in a heavy, 3-quart saucepan. Set it over medium-low heat and stir constantly with a long-handled wooden spoon, until the sugars have dissolved and the mixture begins to boil, 4 to 5 minutes.

Increase the heat to medium-high and put a candy thermometer in the saucepan. Continue to stir until the caramel reaches 240 to 242 degrees F (the soft-ball stage) on the thermometer, about 10 minutes. Remove the pan from the heat and stir in the reserved butter mixture. Stir until it is well combined. Pour the mixture into the prepared baking pan. The caramel will be only about ¼ inch thick. Cool it completely, about 2 hours.

Using the ends of the foil, lift the caramel out of the pan. On a lightly oiled cutting surface, invert the caramel and peel the foil off the back. Oil the blade of a large knife, and cut the caramel into eight 1-inch-wide strips. Re-oil the knife and cut each strip into eight 1-inch-wide pieces. Wrap the caramels individually in 4-by-4-inch waxed paper squares. Store the caramels in an airtight container at room temperature for up to 2 weeks.

MAKES 64 CARAMELS

INDEX

TABLE OF EQUIVALENTS

The exact equivalents in the following tables have been rounded for convenience.

LIQUID/DRY MEASURES

U.S.	METRIC
¼ teaspoon	1.25 milliliters
½ teaspoon	2.5 milliliters
1 teaspoon	5 milliliters
1 tablespoon (3 teaspoons)	15 milliliters
1 fluid ounce (2 tablespoons)	30 milliliters
¼ cup	60 milliliters
⅓ cup	80 milliliters
½ cup	120 milliliters
1 cup	240 milliliters
1 pint (2 cups)	480 milliliters
1 quart (4 cups, 32 ounces)	960 milliliters
1 gallon (4 quarts)	3.84 liters
1 ounce (by weight)	28 grams
1 pound	454 grams
2.2 pounds	1 kilogram

OVEN TEMPERATURE

FAHRENHEIT	CELSIUS	GAS
250	120	½
275	140	1
300	150	2
325	160	3
350	180	4
375	190	5
400	200	6
425	220	7
450	230	8
475	240	9
500	260	10

LENGTH

U.S.	METRIC
⅛ inch	3 millimeters
¼ inch	6 millimeters
½ inch	12 millimeters
1 inch	2.5 centimeters